Implementi

# ChangeSmart™:
## Implementing Change Without Lowering Your Bottom Line

Beth Banks Cohn, Ph.D.

2007

Copyright © 2007 Beth Banks Cohn, Ph.D.
All rights reserved.
ISBN: 1-4196-7398-X
ISBN-13: 978-1419673986

# ChangeSmart™:
Implementing Change Without Lowering Your Bottom Line

# Table of Contents

**Acknowledgments** . . . . . . . . . . . . . . . . . . . . . ix
**Introduction**. . . . . . . . . . . . . . . . . . . . . . . . . xi
**A Framework for Change** . . . . . . . . . . . . . . . 1
**The ChangeSmart™ Framework** . . . . . . . . . . . 3
**Prepare** . . . . . . . . . . . . . . . . . . . . . . . . . . . . . 5
Analyze. . . . . . . . . . . . . . . . . . . . . . . . . . . . . . 6
Understanding the Context. . . . . . . . . . . . . . . . 7
A Tool You Can Use: Create a Map of Change. . . . . . 8
Organizational Readiness. . . . . . . . . . . . . . . . . .10
A Tool You Can Use: Organizational
   Readiness Chart. . . . . . . . . . . . . . . . . . . . .10
Deep Dive: Know Your Leadership . . . . . . . . . . .12
Case in Point: . . . . . . . . . . . . . . . . . . . . . . . . .12
Collaborate . . . . . . . . . . . . . . . . . . . . . . . . . . .16
Feedback Loops . . . . . . . . . . . . . . . . . . . . . . .16
Positive Partings . . . . . . . . . . . . . . . . . . . . . . .18
Case in Point: . . . . . . . . . . . . . . . . . . . . . . . . .18
Plan. . . . . . . . . . . . . . . . . . . . . . . . . . . . . . . .23
Prepare. . . . . . . . . . . . . . . . . . . . . . . . . . . . . .26
Checklist for Success . . . . . . . . . . . . . . . . . . . .26
**Execute**. . . . . . . . . . . . . . . . . . . . . . . . . . . . .27
Engage . . . . . . . . . . . . . . . . . . . . . . . . . . . . . .29
How to Engage You, Let Me Count the Ways . . . . . .29
Case In Point: . . . . . . . . . . . . . . . . . . . . . . . . .30
Another Case In Point: . . . . . . . . . . . . . . . . . . .31
Connect . . . . . . . . . . . . . . . . . . . . . . . . . . . .33
A Tool You Can Use: Conversation Guide . . . . . . . .34
Train . . . . . . . . . . . . . . . . . . . . . . . . . . . . . . .36
Case In Point: . . . . . . . . . . . . . . . . . . . . . . . . .37
Don't Forget about Managers . . . . . . . . . . . . . . .38

| | |
|---|---|
| Case in Point: | 39 |
| Concluding Thoughts | 41 |
| Execute | 42 |
| Checklist for Success | 42 |
| **Sustain** | **45** |
| Align | 47 |
| Case in Point: | 47 |
| Honor the Past to Move to the Future | 48 |
| Measure | 51 |
| Baseline, Baseline, Baseline | 52 |
| Complete | 54 |
| Are We There Yet? | 54 |
| Case in Point: | 55 |
| A Tool You Can Use: Lessons Learned | 57 |
| Sustain | 59 |
| Checklist for Success | 59 |
| **Resistance** | **61** |
| Three Types of Resistance | 62 |
| Blind Resistance | 63 |
| Ideological Resistance | 64 |
| Political Resistance | 65 |
| **Conclusion** | **67** |

# Acknowledgments

This book has been a labor of love from the very beginning. Many years ago, when I stumbled into the world of change management, I knew that I had found my calling. For almost twenty years I have helped companies make the changes they've needed to remain viable, and I have had a ton of fun in the process.

The biggest lesson I have learned, which I try to share on the following pages, is this: When a change goes well, there is a positive ripple effect that reverberates and brings more and more positive energy, like a pebble dropped in a pond. The opposite is also true, and that is where companies struggle.

There are so many people who have touched my life on my travels through the hallways of corporate America. You are too numerous to mention, but I thank all of you for your guidance and engagement.

I'd like to express my gratitude and love to my husband, Jules, for all his guidance and support. I could not have done this without him.

I dedicate this book to two very special people: to the late Ralph Ganger, who gave me my start and encouraged me to go after my dreams, and to the late Dr. Libby Douvan without whom I would not have finished my dissertation and found my voice. I hope they knew how I felt about them when they were alive. They continue to influence me to this day.

# Introduction

There have been hundreds of books written on change and change management. Each one claims to take the mystery and the misery out of the process. In many ways they do and are very helpful—if you are in the change management business. But most people who need to know the best ways to manage through change are business people, where change is inevitable, but it isn't what you sell or produce. As business people we want to improve our bottom line through change, not change for the sake of it or spend too much time and energy on it.

Change management is about helping organizations move to their desired state through people. The best spreadsheets in the world can't make a change work; although they are often at the root of the decision. It is your employees, and the actions they take, that will make or break a change. That is true power. Change management is about connecting to that power, the power of your employees, to effect transformation.

On the following pages, you will be introduced to a framework called ChangeSmart™. ChangeSmart™ is a way to approach change that was developed over many years, through work on many projects—some successful, some not—inside several corporations. It is a roadmap for success. It isn't a model; it is a set of ideas to help you implement your new business strategies with the intended results.

I have used this framework successfully in sales, marketing, customer service, manufacturing, research and finance organizations. I have used it successfully in large companies and small start-ups. Sometimes the changes were quite significant and required the use of all these tools, and more, to be successful. Sometimes the changes were just in leadership or a small contained process where only parts of this roadmap were needed.

Use what works for you in the context of your unique project. Scale the time and energy you expend to the size of your venture.

***A word to the wise:*** If your change is big, affecting many groups, with a big price tag and/or a big ROI expected, you may want to seek the help of a change management specialist. Good, effective change management isn't as easy as it looks. If you work in a large corporation, you may be lucky enough to have those people on staff. If not, look to the outside. At the very least, they can be an extra pair of hands that will prove invaluable over time.

If your change is small and you feel confident you and your team can handle the change component, I encourage you to give one person overall responsibility for change management, and then use this book to guide your way. Not all the tools will be as useful for small changes, but remember that small is a relative word. Your small change may be coming on the heels of several major changes, and like it or not, you will be affected by them.

Even if you implement one tool or idea from this book to start, you will improve the quality of your results. Always strive for continual progress, not the perfect implementation, and you will do well.

As you know, there is no silver bullet to successfully implementing changes into an organization. It takes an understanding of how your change fits into the business, attention, good timing and follow-through. When it comes to implementing new business initiatives, there are ***many right ways*** to approach it. I encourage you to use the ideas on the following pages to enhance your approach.

Change comes at organizations and individuals with blinding speed. Most change is internally driven, although some of it is driven by their chosen marketplace. Either way, change is a fact of life today in business, but that doesn't always make it easier to carry out successfully.

I am not going to tell you to rethink the pace of change in your company, although you could. Nor will I tell you that change is good and should be embraced by all. It isn't. Change is neither bad nor good—it just is. It is one's reaction to change, the way one manages oneself, and sometimes others, through change, which makes the experience bad or good.

You will have the most success using this book if you remain open to the results you experience. If something doesn't work the way you thought it would, that is an opportunity for learning, not a reason to stop trying new things. This book was written to help you, the business person, navigate through change in a productive way, so you can remain focused on your business. It was written to help you connect with your most important asset during your initiative, your employees, the people it affects.

*"It is your employees, and the actions they take, that will make or break a change."*

# A Framework for Change

I am often asked what "change model" I use when I help an organization prepare for change. I must confess that I don't use any model in particular, although many influence the work that I do. Models are great, but they are often difficult to translate into an effective process for each unique change. Processes are fine, but they often denote a rigid set of steps one must follow. ChangeSmart™ is a framework for change. It will fit with any model you use, any process you choose to follow. It takes into account the uniqueness of each change. There are many ways to make a change successful. The key is to pick the way that will work best for your organization and the individuals in it. ChangeSmart™ is a framework that, if followed, will focus your energy on the right actions to take to ensure your business's success.

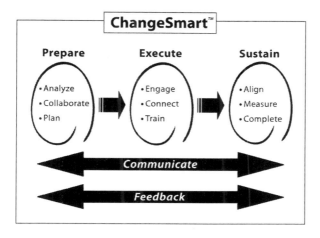

# The ChangeSmart™ Framework

The ChangeSmart™ Framework has three main elements: Prepare, Execute and Sustain. In addition, there are two core topics that run through all three elements: Communication and Feedback.

Although each element works best as part of the entire framework, feel free to use different pieces alone. Don't allow yourself to be overwhelmed. Pick one thing to do differently, try it, and then when you are successful, pick something else to try. Remember, continual progress is your goal.

The ChangeSmart™ framework fits well within any project plan. It can be the glue that binds all the disparate pieces together. Integrate the steps you choose into the overall project plan. This allows change management outcomes to be viewed by everyone involved and gives everyone clear context for the actions to be taken.

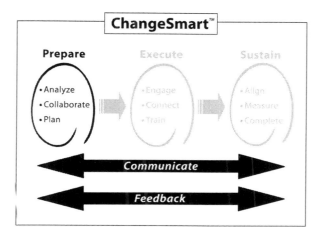

# Prepare

Preparation is the important first step a company takes after deciding to implement something new. Ideally the groundwork begins while the management team is deciding upon the initiative, but at the very least, once the decision is made the work should begin. There are three major components to the Prepare element: Analyze, Collaborate and Plan.

The Analyze component is the most important part of the Prepare element. Unfortunately, it is the part where eyes start glazing over and people tend to want to skip to the next part. I understand you want to get started; you don't want to dwell on the past. After all, you aren't going to be measured on how well you understand the context and environment surrounding the change. Or are you?

Failure to consider the current business environment may yield less than anticipated results. Your plan will simply not be the right one. People will work very hard executing against a plan that will not get you to your defined success. At the end of the project when the results are not achieved, you will question why and receive many answers: the market changed, the business changed, the employees didn't do what they were supposed to, the project team didn't focus on the right things. There will be an element of truth in all of them, and it can be tied back to a failure to analyze and take into consideration the internal and external environment.

Pay attention to the next section, the Analyze section. When your eyes start glazing over, come back to this section to remind yourself why it is important.

## Analyze

Analyze is where you gather information that will be the foundation of your actions during the Execute and Sustain elements of the ChangeSmart™ framework. It is essential, before you start any change, that you:

- Understand the context or the environment in which you are pursuing this initiative;
- Comprehend your organization's readiness;
- Know the level of your leadership's support

## Understanding the Context

A critical piece of information when making plans is to understand the organizational environment into which the change is being introduced. It is important to identify what other initiatives have gone on in the organization during the last twelve months, and what was and is their ongoing effect.

The number of initiatives, the depth of the changes associated with them, the number of people affected, whether the other changes included reorganizations or layoffs will all impact an organization's ability to successfully internalize another change.

This isn't a discussion about whether the "timing is right" for a new business initiative. The timing is rarely "right." But it is important to consider whether the organization will be able to implement what is planned and achieve the desired results. The environment is rarely as prepared as it could be or as ready as it needs to be. Understanding all of that in the context of your organization is vital to the success of your initiative.

Always keep in mind that there is a limit to how much change an organization, and the people in it, can bear before success is negatively impacted. It may be easy to dismiss this idea, but it has the potential to cost millions of dollars in both productivity and revenue if not given due consideration. If you've implemented six changes in the last year that included reorganizations and a few layoffs, you need to include the impact of them in your plans.

I'm not going to recommend that you slow down your pace as you try to transform your business. I will just ask you to consider this question: If you are making that many changes, of that magnitude, in that timeframe, are you really giving anything a chance to work?

# A Tool You Can Use: Create a Map of Change

A map of change will give you a visual representation of all the changes that have gone on in your organization over the last year. This "picture" will help you understand the environment into which you are introducing your initiative.

Follow these steps to create your map:

1. Using butcher block paper on a conference room or office wall, create a timeline of the last year and the coming year.

2. Put all the changes that have been made underneath the timeline, drawing a line to show the beginning and the end.

    - Include all initiatives, whether they were company-wide or departmental.

3. Underneath every initiative list the departments involved, how many people were affected, and identify the number of systems or processes that were impacted.

    - You could color code this information based on a Small, Medium or Large scale if you so desire.

4. Now put your planned change on the timeline and fill in the same information.

Take a step back from your map and look at what has taken place. Note the sizes of the changes and the number of people and processes involved as well as the timing over the year.

Now consider your planned change and record the following on a separate flipchart:

- What Departments
- What Systems
- What Processes

are going to be affected by this upcoming change that have been affected in the last year by other initiatives ***and how many times***.

Now you have the information you need to plan for your new initiative. Use this information as input into your change management and change communication plans.

For example, a department that has been through a few other changes in the past year will need you to spell out how your change fits in with all the others. This may require creating a conversation guide for managers as well as having senior management or team leadership address it during a company meeting. If the other changes haven't had good communication, it will be extremely important for your project to have exemplary communication to counteract the damage that was caused.

***A word to the wise:*** If the employees in your company, or a division or department have been through many changes in the last year, they aren't "used to it" by now—they are tired. Plan accordingly.

### *Middle Management Alert*

What if you are a director or manager or a team leader but aren't on the team implementing the change? You can still use this tool to be prepared for how this change may affect your group. Record the same information focusing on just your department. Include employee turnover and leadership changes as well on your map. You may find that one small group of employees is more affected than others, or you may find that your whole team is in the same place. Whatever you find, weave that into your own plans as you implement the current initiative.

**Organizational Readiness**

A lot of analysis was probably done when deciding to take on a new business initiative, but one set of analysis is usually missing—understanding the organization's readiness to successfully implement the change. The Change Map you created will be important information that feeds into your discussion of organizational readiness, but there are additional factors to consider. Is the organization itself—the Leadership, People, Processes, Policies and Culture—ready to make the change?

**A Tool You Can Use: Organizational Readiness Chart**

In order to answer the question "Are we ready to make this change?" list the Departments being affected on a flipchart. Also list the Systems (computer or otherwise) and Processes that are changing. Create several additional categories called People, Leadership, Resources, Structure, Policies and Culture.

Think about each department, system, process and the other listed categories and ask yourself the following questions: If this business initiative were being implemented tomorrow, would this category be:

- An enabler of the change?
- A barrier to the change?
- A potential enabler, but needs special attention?

Assign a letter (E, B, S) or a color (Green, Red, Yellow seem to work well) to each category. A majority of E's or greens indicates you have the basis for a successful change. A majority of S's or yellows or a majority of B's or reds indicates you need to pay careful attention to those areas. You can move ahead with your plans, even with a majority of S's or B's—you just need to plan for it. No matter what the mix of E's, B's or S's, make sure a plan is in place to support those business realities.

*Example:*

## Organizational Readiness

KEY  E=Enabler  B=Barrier  S=Special Attention

| Department 1 | E |
|---|---|
| Department 2 | E |
| Department 3 | B |
| System 1 | B |
| Process 1 | S |
| Process 2 | S |
| People | E |
| Leadership | E |
| Resources | S |
| Structure | B |
| Policies | S |
| Culture | E |

Don't create this list and then put the results in a drawer. This isn't a box to check. It is a vital piece of information that should be used to help you manage through the planned change. Review this information periodically; update it as necessary and then modify your plan accordingly.

*Middle Management Alert*

This same tool can help you as the leader of a team or department about to go through a change, even if you aren't leading the initiative. Honestly assess your department in terms of Systems, Processes, People, Leadership, Resources, Structure and Culture. Don't make it complicated, just think about it or talk about it with a colleague, and record your ratings. Use it to help you remain aware of potential issues as you move through the change.

### Deep Dive: Know Your Leadership

It will also be important as you Analyze your organization to make sure you know which specific members of your senior management team are enablers, on the fence or barriers to success. Even though you decided whether your leadership was an enabler or a barrier ***in general*** during the Organizational Readiness discussion, it will be important to take this one step further and discuss each individual.

Make a list of each person on the senior management team and have a discussion about where you think he or she fits. Use the same categories—enabler, barrier or potential enabler. Again, you can make the change with leaders scattered in all three positions, you just have to be prepared for it.

Just that information will be helpful as you move forward with your plans. If you really want to know your leadership, record what makes them an enabler, a barrier or a potential enabler. Are they an enabler because they truly understand the potential of this business initiative? Are they a barrier because they will not free up resources critical to the project? Do they need special attention because they say they support you, but they don't act like they do? Knowing this type of information will help you formulate good plans to move leaders from potential enablers or barriers to enablers.

***A word to the wise:*** Be brutally honest in these discussions. Nothing but a ***true*** evaluation will give you information that will help move your project forward.

*Case in Point:* A $4 billion dollar pharmaceutical company with over one thousand sales representatives was poised to implement both a new selling process and a new computer system at the same time. The goal was to work more effectively with customers and translate that into higher sales.

The sales force was a mix of tenured and just-out-of-college representatives. All had the science backgrounds needed to sell their sophisticated line of drugs. Field sales management had come up through the ranks and had been in the industry a long time.

Although company leadership had overall agreed that this project made sense, there were one or two members of the senior leadership team who were still not convinced of the project's merits.

Early on, the project team identified some key company leaders as barriers. The team identified those leaders they wanted to move from "potential enablers" or "barriers" to "enablers." Throughout the first months of the project, the team leader met periodically with those identified, talking with them about the change, soliciting their opinions, keeping them informed of the team's progress. Some company leaders moved from "potential enablers" to "enablers," some moved from "barriers" to "potential enablers," some didn't move at all.

When implementation day came and problems started to arise—as often happens when new technologies are involved—the project team was delighted to find that some of their key leaders who had turned from "potential enablers" to "enablers" really helped them through the critical startup phase. This didn't just happen by chance; this happened because of the work the team leader and the team did with those individuals. This proved critical in solving the issues that arose while maintaining the support of everyone involved. The team leader didn't sit on his laurels; he continued to work with those company leaders to ensure they stayed as "enablers" all the way through. This was not always easy work, but it payed off in the way the technology was used to enhance sales—one of the main goals of the project.

Unfortunately, some leaders that remained "barriers" continued to be "barriers" through the end. Team leadership became frustrated and stopped trying to convince these "barriers" to support the work of the project. In fact, even today, years after the project was completed, some of those leaders still consider it a failure.

There were many lessons to be learned from this scenario. There are degrees of "barrier," and it is worth understanding that as plans are made. If you can't move someone from being a "barrier" to an "enabler," then it will be important to manage your relationship with him or her very closely as the project progresses. As tempting as it is, don't just walk away from your "barriers." Stick with them until their objections cease to be relevant any more—because you've successfully implemented the change.

*"If the employees...have been through many changes in the last year, they aren't "used to it" by now—they are tired. Plan accordingly"*

# Notes

# Collaborate

It is important during the preparation stage to encourage not only the team to work together but also those affected. The change may have been announced "with more info to follow," and it is a good time to engage those affected. You may want to create sub-teams, or you may want to run focus groups — the possibilities are only limited by your interest. Collaboration helps fuel the positive aspects of the change. Even when there is a negative or downside to the change, encouraging collaboration between individuals helps blunt the effects.

Oftentimes project team members get so involved in their work that they forget to engage others early in the process. "We're not ready yet" is a statement I often hear. It is just when a team feels they aren't "ready" that they need to reach out. It is never too early to ask what people think or engage others in some way. It is also a way to help people begin to make the mind shifts necessary instead of waiting to spring everything on them at once.

Sometimes a team will say they don't have the time, they have deadlines to meet and too much work to complete. It is understandable, but the time invested in engaging others outside of the team will give a great rate of return on the investment later.

### Feedback Loops

Feedback loops are an easy way to involve others outside the project team while continuing to move the project forward. Simply put, a feedback loop is a formalized process of gathering people's opinions and giving people information about the project's progress.

Feedback loops give people an opportunity to voice their thoughts about the planned change before it happens as well as how it is progressing after implementation. Your feedback loops will be your lifeline, in effect, and are an essential part of any change process. Who you involve and what you ask may change through the life of your project, but the consistency of having a feedback loop will carry you far.

Feedback is best given and received in person. Videoconferencing or phone conferences are best after that. This is where your project change management consultants—internal or external—can really come in handy as that extra pair of hands. They can conduct the focus groups, take notes, write up and analyze the results and suggest possible actions.

Written surveys are the least effective way to receive feedback and are frequently frustrating for both the writer and the receiver of the information. With written surveys incomplete information is often given and received, thereby lowering the chances of any action being taken. I only recommend written surveys when geography and size of the population make other types of feedback difficult to manage. Questions with little ambiguity and/or the ability to write in comments are the key to successfully using written surveys.

*A word to the wise:* Don't just go through the motions of asking what people think. If you set up opportunities for people to give feedback and simply ignore what they have to say, you will cause more damage than not having asked them at all. People don't expect leadership to take all of their advice, but they do expect consideration for what they have to say if their opinions are solicited. Part of a successful feedback loop process is letting folks know they've been heard and what you will and won't be doing as a result.

### *Middle Management Alert*

If you have the opportunity to participate in a feedback

session during this process, take advantage of it. Encourage your staff to do the same. If no feedback loops are offered, suggest them to the team leaders. If your request falls on deaf ears, use the feedback loop model on a small scale in your department or team. It will allow you to keep close tabs on how your team is faring and bring issues to the forefront before they become problems.

**Positive Partings**

Be realistic. If you know 20% of your work force is going to lose their jobs through this change, don't make a big show of including everyone in the preparation for it. Use that reality to set the stage for "positive partings." How a company treats those who will leave it during a reduction in force will directly affect how successful the change ultimately is. Business transformation often requires the reallocation of resources; everyone knows this. How a company handles that "reallocation" is what people react to—positively or negatively.

*Case in Point:* A large corporation with ten thousand employees announced a change that was to affect approximately 30% of specific department employees with the loss of their jobs. Others would be demoted or reassigned outside of their current area. This was a big change for many people. Some (amazingly enough) had never experienced anything like this in their tenure with the company.

This company had a reputation for fairness and for caring for employees, but during this change there was limited communication about the timelines for these decisions. Even as individuals were told their jobs were eliminated, there was no help immediately available in finding other jobs. Longevity had been valued at this company, so many people with 10 or more years of employment lost their jobs and this hit everyone hard.

During previous changes, elsewhere in the corporation, which resulted in reductions in the workforce, severance had been higher than what was being offered during this initiative. There was a general perception that those let go were not respected for what they had contributed during their tenure. Those being let go felt slighted and devalued. They left the company with large amounts of organizational knowledge still tucked safely away in their heads. They had no incentive or mechanism to share that organizational knowledge with others before they took their leave.

All in all, the employees that kept their jobs were not only upset about their own situation of fewer people doing more work, but they were even more upset by the way they perceived their peers were being treated. The loss in productivity and morale created a work situation that lacked energy and creativity.

Three years later, this company still struggles to meet its business goals. The company no longer enjoys the reputation it once had, which makes it hard to recruit and harder to keep employees. The actions the company didn't take are a good example of something I often say: *"Change handled badly is never over."*

And that simply translates into lost opportunity and lost revenue. This situation could have easily been avoided by treating employees consistent with the culture, and with dignity and respect as they walked through the door for the very last time.

A communication plan could have been created and carried out with the concerns of the employees in mind. Communication consistent with the culture of caring and compassion would have gone a long way to heal the hurt that people were feeling. This means acknowledging the pain layoffs were going to bring and reiterating why the company had made that difficult decision.

These things are simple to do yet often overlooked as each senior manager looks to someone else to do them.

Sadly, this company will probably not consider their past actions in this area when they search for the reasons their business is still struggling. That is unfortunate but not uncommon, and it creates a downward spiral affect. The company hasn't learned the real reasons for their business downturns. They make more changes to fix their 'problem,' but it doesn't seem to work. So they make more changes...get the picture? If a company considers *all* possibilities when a business initiative doesn't work as anticipated, it can make corrections successfully. Remember, it is the people side of change that causes a change to succeed or fail. A company that won't consider their own internal actions as part of the reason for failure is a company that will continue to struggle.

*"Change handled badly is never over."*

### Middle Management Alert

If you have employees that are being separated as part of a change initiative make sure they leave on as good terms as possible. If they have been given time to find a new job and will still be using their workspace, don't ignore them. Of course you have business to attend to, but that doesn't mean you can't continue to check in with them and see how their job search is going. Before they leave for the last time, make sure to thank them for their contributions on behalf of yourself, *and the company,* and wish them well. After all, you are management and can speak as a representative of the company in this instance. It doesn't make up for their job loss at all, but it allows them to leave with dignity. Besides being the right thing to do, it will help your employees that remain with the company to move through the change positively.

# Notes

# Plan

Have a Plan, Work the Plan

To you are clear about your readiness, and you've decided what you will do to enhance or maintain it. You've also decided how to include and engage people through collaborative efforts. Now you need to write it all down in a formal plan. You might be tempted to skip this component. After all, you know what you want to do, but it is important for continuity and consistency that you create a formal change management plan.

The change plan should include not only all the tasks that will be done in support of this change but also who will do them, who the target audience is, what the goal is and the due date. Don't forget to include all communications and all training. Don't underestimate the importance of having everything you are doing in support of the change written down and assigned.

Change management is not the responsibility of one individual or even a project team, but rather the entire organization. However, someone needs to be responsible for driving it. The role that company leadership and the project team plays in a change can mean the difference between success and failure. In addition, make sure your plan includes what you are doing in each part of the framework— Prepare, Execute and Sustain.

Keep in mind that the plan should include your ideas for dealing with any issues that come up as you implement the change. Use the Map of Change and your Organizational Readiness information to generate what those issues might be and what you will do about them. And remember, ***then a miracle occurs and then the problem is solved*** is not a realistic task on the project plan—although many organizations seem to employ it.

Organizations often forget that in order for a change to

really be successful everyone needs to continue working on the change well after the implementation date. Some changes will be adapted quickly, others not. If you have done your analysis, you'll know how your change is being assimilated. Your feedback loops will keep you updated, and your plan will keep you focused.

You may ask how long to keep these kinds of activities going after the "go live" date. My rule of thumb is six months. It can be less, it can be more—your analysis and focus groups will tell you on what end of the time spectrum you should be.

I can hear you saying to yourself: "Are you kidding? Who can keep a project team in place for that long? People move on." I agree, and it is part of the challenge, but finding a creative way to keep people engaged until the project is really over will be a critical success factor. There will be more on this topic later under the Execute element.

Remember, as boring as it sounds, creating your plan and working your plan will lead you to success.

*"Availability is not a job skill..."*

# Notes

# Prepare

# Checklist for Success

*Use this checklist to make sure you have done everything possible to set yourself up for success in the early stages of your project.*

- We understand the context or environment into which we are introducing our change.

- We know our organization's readiness to accept this change and have planned accordingly.

- We know our leadership's support of this initiative and have implemented the necessary steps to make the desired changes.

- We have designed different ways to engage those affected by this initiative, including feedback loops.

- If layoffs or reallocation of resources is involved, we have a plan that includes attention to both those who stay and those who will leave.

- We have an integrated project plan that includes all activities, including those specific to change management and change communication.

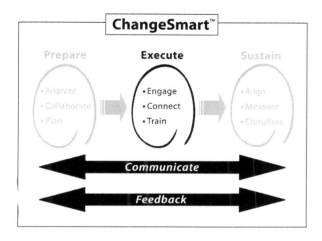

# Execute

The Execute part of the ChangeSmart™ framework isn't simply implementing the change, flipping the switch, and then walking away. Execute represents all those things you need to do around the change to make sure it is successful. There is an attention to detail necessary during Execute that requires:

- Engagement of all employees, not just the project team

- Measuring Success

- Closing the Project Down

Just as everyone has a role in the success of the business, everyone also has a role in the success of a change to that business.

I have worked with many companies who assemble what they consider great teams, create intricate and detailed project plans and then don't execute against them. Execution, or as I like to say, doing the work, is critical. When you are making up your project team, make sure it is populated with individuals who can execute, not just plan and direct others to do the actual work.

Populate the team with leaders people will willingly follow. Don't use a project like this as a developmental opportunity for team leaders who struggle with getting things done through others. Or if you do, at least make sure they have a coach to walk with them every step of the way.

When populating a cross-functional team, remember that 'availability' is not a job skill. Be clear about what skills an individual must possess to be on the project team. As much as you can, set the team up for success before they ever begin.

Execution is also about organizational attention span. If your company has trouble sustaining interest in something longer than a few months, don't create a project that will take 18 months to complete. Create several smaller projects that take a few months each—it will work out much better for all involved.

The last key to success is senior management backing. A team will only execute well if it knows someone in senior management cares and continues to pay attention. Keeping senior management engaged and supportive is a joint responsibility between the team leadership and senior management itself, and it is an important part of project execution.

# Engage

So the day is finally here; today you are starting to implement the business initiative you have been working on. If you haven't already been engaging all those affected by this initiative, now is not too late. People may be unsure of themselves and where they fit in with all the changes. They may be enthusiastic but rudderless. All the factors you thought about during the Prepare element—organizational readiness, the context and magnitude of the change—come into play here. It is essential to engage people immediately or risk losing them.

A time of change affects different people in different ways. This is a time when some people may choose to withdraw into themselves. They may be creating an emotional distance which they think will help them weather this latest "storm." That doesn't mean that emotions are bad and should be suppressed. On the contrary, emotions are an important part of any change process. But by engaging people in the change, allowing them to fully participate, you can help them start creating their new reality sooner.

Whether you ask them their opinion through a focus group or their manager makes time to talk with them, engaging individuals throughout the process will be a critical success factor. This work continues all through Execute and into Sustain. If you start engaging people in the Plan element, it will be easier to continue that all the way through until the end. But even if you don't, it is not too late to start during the Execute element. Just don't forget to carry it through.

### How to Engage You, Let Me Count the Ways

As a project team, brainstorm all the potential ways to engage people throughout the change process. The project team isn't the only group of people who can reach out and connect with people. If the change affects the whole company, that also means that every senior leader and every people manager can play a part. In addition, don't forget your "informal" leaders—those individuals whom people follow even though they may not have a formal leadership position. Those individuals need to be both engaged and to engage others. Their role can be very important.

Even though I have already mentioned managers, it is worth mentioning them again. Your middle managers will be the difference between the success and the failure of your business initiative. I am sometimes amazed how many team leaders, middle managers themselves, forget to engage their peers. Engage them, work with them, utilize their expertise, and it will go well. Ignore them, alienate them, try to work around them, and the results will be disastrous.

Managers are the individuals responsible for making the day-to-day operations of the business proceed as necessary. When a change is implemented, the organization looks to the managers to be their "man or woman in the field." Yet they are often forgotten and overlooked. When discussing ways of engaging employees, have a special plan for engaging managers. Whether it is creating a manager advisory committee or conducting special briefings on the project's progress, whatever you can do to include this group will relate directly to the change's success.

*Case In Point:* A large manufacturing plant with two thousand employees, running three shifts, needed to implement a sweeping change in how production was planned, how products were manufactured and how they traveled through their different manufacturing locations. As the team planned the project, they left out a very important group of individuals—the floor supervisors. These managers were left in the dark for most of the project until it came time to implement the new processes. In discussions with the project team, it became clear that there were big gaps in understanding the capabilities that existed on the manufacturing floor which would potentially cause the changes to fail.

The supervisors didn't agree with some of the proposed changes based on their knowledge of their part of the business. They pointed out issues the project team hadn't considered, or had dismissed as minor. If the changes were implemented as designed, the supervisors foresaw a host of problems from misinformation in the new computer system to slowdowns in production.

In the face of potentially huge monetary losses, the project team was forced to rework some of their plans. This time, however, they learned from their mistake and engaged the floor supervisors in the rework. The result was a much smoother transition and immediate uptake of the required changes. The mistake of not engaging a key management group cost the company money, but it was nothing compared to the millions in lost revenue it could have cost if the mistakes were not corrected prior to implementation.

The project team's mistake was clear, but it was puzzling to the team leaders because they had people on the team with supervisory experience. It was a good lesson learned to engage people who are currently doing the job because their issues and difficulties are constantly in their mind.

*Another Case In Point:* A five hundred person sales force was poised to implement a new approach to selling that would require major changes in how sales representatives planned their sales calls, the language they used with their customers and the kind of follow-up they provided. Knowing the district managers were critical partners in making this initiative stick, the project team and sales leadership devised a plan early on how to engage them.

The plan included extensive briefings and training on the initiative as it progressed. The managers were the first to know about everything. The methods were piloted, and the managers involved shared their insights with the other managers so they could learn from each others' experiences. Each district manager was also asked to make sure their representatives completed the required training and had a certain level of knowledge before the rollout.

During the training, where the whole program was rolled out to the entire sales force, the district managers were asked to play a training and coaching role. They also received prior training and support to fulfill those roles, including how to deal with resistance and over-enthusiasm out in the field.

After the rollout, each district manager was asked to ride with each of their representatives once in the first three weeks to review their understanding and use of their new skills, and make course corrections as necessary. This was difficult for some managers to do because of the geography of their districts, but everyone did their best to fulfill this request.

Each week during the first three months, the managers talked weekly with their regional business director and each other to highlight successes and solve issues. The calls weren't long, but they were very helpful and gave great support to the managers. In addition, focus groups were conducted for a subset of the managers, where they could freely give their feedback on how the changes were being implemented.

Because the district managers were engaged from the very beginning, both with information and support, it was natural for them to accept their critical role in the process. None of this happened by chance. The pre-work the managers did with their staff, the post-implementation follow up, the weekly calls and the focus groups were all part of the project plan. The team simply executed against it.

The implementation had its desired result and met its goals easily. All thanks to the attention paid by the project team to the critical manager role.

*"Your middle managers will be the difference between success and failure..."*

## Connect

During a change effort there is a need to help people make the connection between what they did before and what they need to do now. This is often overlooked as the company and the project team looks forward to what the world will be like after the change. Many a project team forgets that they too went through the searching conversations and thought processes about how what they currently do will relate to what they will need to do. They've just gone through it about six months earlier. A highly effective project team will realize that everyone else is going to need to go through the same thing and be prepared for it.

## A Tool You Can Use: Conversation Guide

One way of helping individuals through this process is to create a conversation guide for managers to use with their staffs. These conversation guides can include questions to ask individuals during one-on-ones or questions to ask during staff meetings to help the process along. In addition, the changes can be laid out simply with a "before" and "after" picture that will help managers explain the change again to their staffs. There can also be a section on what to stop doing or what to do differently and why.

Potential headings in a conversation guide can be:

- How to Use This Guide
- When to Use This Guide
- Where do I go for more information?
- Initiative Overview
- Overview of Changes
- Specific Changes (may differ by department)

You may also want to include support materials for the manager like an overview of the stages of change or how to handle resistance—whatever you feel is appropriate for your situation.

Individuals will be searching for answers and will find them either through their formal or informal networks. When time and accuracy is of the essence, it will be important to support managers and employees with this type of formal information.

Many individuals will also need to adjust their work identity to align with the change. Oftentimes, it is when individuals can't see themselves in the newly re-organized company that they resign—either in place or by leaving the company.

Moving on to another opportunity outside of the

department or the company isn't necessarily a bad thing, but it often happens with the employees you'd most like to keep at a time you'd really like to keep them. Resigning in place is a most dangerous occurrence for both the individual and the company. This is when people go through the motions of their work but don't bring their creativity and intelligence to it anymore. Either scenario does not help make your business initiative successful.

You can leave people to figure out how the change affects them on their own, or you can help it along. Just remember, the sooner individuals see themselves in the new organization, the sooner the drop in productivity and the potential for a drop in the bottom line will disappear. This can be true for a small change as well as a large one. When a member of senior management tells me a change is "small," I always like to ask—for whom? Sometimes "small" for the company is "big" for the individual. And sometimes the opposite can also be true. Creating a smooth work identity transition will eliminate both the drop in productivity and the bottom line.

### *Middle Management Alert*

Even if the change implementation team hasn't created a conversation guide you can create one for your own use. Follow the same steps scaled to your department or team, utilize the project team to get the answers you need and begin! You don't even have to write everything down, although it might be helpful over time. Just create an outline of topics you want to cover with each employee, set up your department meeting and enjoy the ensuing conversations.

## Train

Companies usually do a good job at training people on new skills. Although many times the company underestimates the time it will take someone to learn something new. When an executive says "teach them what they need to know in ½ day" and you know it will take at least five times that, it is in the best interest of the project and the company that you speak up.

Often executives don't have a good feel for what really is changing down to the individual level. From where they sit the change is usually quite simple and therefore shouldn't need a lot of retraining. But frequently they are quite open to other opinions, especially from the project team. You are on the ground and have a clearer picture of what it will take for someone to be successful with the change. It is up to you to come up with a training plan that sets the company and the employees up for success.

Of course, sometimes an executive may simply only want to spend a ½ day for monetary or perceived lost productivity reasons. It is then up to the project team to figure out what needs to happen before and after to make the most of that ½ day they have been allotted.

Business realities may preclude you from conducting all the training you would like before the implementation date. Creatively working in additional training before and after that should be part of your plan. When faced with time and resource constraints, ask yourselves the following question: "What does this employee need to know on Monday morning in order to work productively in the new world?" Notice that I don't ask what he or she will need to know in six months to be successful, but what he or she needs to know Monday morning to work and be productive. Sometimes that helps marry the expectations of executives with the realities of the project team.

*Case In Point:* A quality management division that supported five manufacturing locations in a regulated industry needed to make some changes. Both their processes and computer systems were old and needed updating. They were interested in changing how they kept records of issues they encountered in order to make reporting to the federal government more efficient.

The project team had their work cut out for them. They knew they had to change a set of business processes that had been in place for decades and that wouldn't be easy. The project team erred on the side of over-involvement and engaged as many quality associates as they could in reworking the processes. Members of the core project team, which included quality leaders from each manufacturing location in addition to the corporate offices, met often. Additional sub-teams were set up to tackle various issues related to the new processes. The core project team agreed not to begin design of a computer system until the new processes were complete.

The computer system design also included as many associates as possible. Instead of slowing the design process down, it actually allowed them to quickly identify the requirements the systems people needed to create the computer system.

Once the computer system was complete, training needed to take place. Even though many employees had been involved in the design of the new process and system, everyone went through a formal training process. This allowed everyone, even people who had worked on the project, to understand all of the changes that were made, not just the part they worked on. As with the project, process training took place first and then the computer system was introduced. This helped put the entire quality process in context and helped people learn the computer system faster. The project team even conducted briefings for those employees in the manufacturing plants who wouldn't need to use the system but needed to know about the changes in the quality processes.

The whole implementation, which in the end was a sweeping change to the quality processes of the company, was a non-event. The process changes caused no disruptions to the business, the quality group was able to add value to the manufacturing process and the new processes were accepted and implemented without question. Were there things that didn't go as planned? Were there computer issues? Of course, but they were minor and easily corrected. This was a result of the right engagement at the right time, good communication and well planned and appropriate training.

Because the project team engaged so many of those affected by the changes all along the way, the training and, as a result, the time it took to make the changes "business as usual" were streamlined. Every location had representation on the team, so it was easy during the early days to get issues resolved and questions answered in a timely manner. This change affected a small number of people across a wide geographic area. The team took that into consideration all along the way and planned for it. Their structure and plan may not work for your unique situation, but the framework they used certainly can.

### Don't Forget about Managers

It is important in the training plan to include time for training managers. Even if they have received training on change management before, a refresher may be warranted. At the very least, conduct a manager's meeting that gives them an opportunity to work through and resolve issues that may come up within their groups. This saves time and costly missteps in the long run. In addition, giving them additional skills such as recognizing and handling resistance or how to manage through a positive change can help make them better managers for their people and for the company.

As has been mentioned, managers are your keys to success in any change, whether it be with a corporate group or a field force. Don't neglect them or assume they will be on board, just because you tell them to be. It is also important that they know more than their employees about the change.

Make sure you train managers separately and before their employees go through training. That way they can play a leadership role as their employees are being trained. They can't do that if they are trying to learn at the same time in the same training class. Make a special effort to engage them, perhaps piloting the training with them, getting their feedback and making changes accordingly. Don't underestimate the power of this group. Many a change has failed because this group was neglected and not engaged.

*Case in Point:* A company with 6,000 employees was rolling out a new computer system to its employees. All employees went through training, but there was no special training for the managers. Sometimes they went through the training with their employees, sometimes before and sometimes after. Since they often were the last to see the new system, they were powerless to reinforce what their employees learned or support the new way of doing things.

The system was not embraced as it could have been, and technical problems plagued the implementation, not because there were so many technical issues with the system, but because when employees went to their manager with a system issue after implementation, the manager had no knowledge or tools to manage the problems. All issues were escalated with a "the system isn't working again" attitude. In fact, many of the issues were simple process and operator glitches. But because the managers were not included earlier, they had neither the knowledge nor the commitment to see it any other way. The company was plagued with "the system doesn't work right" issues years after implementation. That affected productivity, morale and creativity. All of which directly impacts the bottom line.

What could the project team have done differently? Two things immediately come to mind: The first is that they could have trained the managers prior to the general rollout. Not only could they know more than their employees about the system, but they could also have seen what typical problems might be and questions to ask the employees to help them solve their problems. This may have incurred a monetary cost, but it would have saved them money on the flipside by mitigating the time spent by employees not working, trying to solve their own problems and calling the help desk. They also could have designated a specialist for each work area and trained them earlier as well. In this company a computer specialists program was in place, it just needed to be expanded.

Secondly, the project team could have engaged the managers after the initial rollout as well. Giving all the managers an ongoing voice into what was working well and what wasn't would have helped them become more efficient faster. Giving structure to feedback sessions would have prevented the complaining that did take place whenever people were asked "how it was going." Sharing successes and best practices would have also increased their team's usage of the tools and given some balance to the positive and negative aspects of such an initiative.

### *Middle Management Alert*

If your employees aren't getting the training you think they need to do their jobs you have two choices: 1. get someone to provide it for you, or 2. provide it yourself. Or get creative and ask high performing employees to mentor those taking a little longer to catch on. Set up a weekly review session to emphasize important topics and give people a chance to problem solve issues. None of these activities needs to last indefinitely. Earmark the first month or two after a change for these types of actions. As a result, your group's productivity will remain consistent throughout the implementation.

## Concluding Thoughts

Execution isn't that hard, but it is often where companies stumble. If your company has a history of faulty execution, it is worth taking into consideration as you plan your project. Three ways to help execution along are to:

- engage everyone affected in the process,
- help individuals and groups make the connections between the old way and the new one, and
- give everyone affected the training they need to be successful.

I will say it again; I would shout it from the rooftops if I thought it would make a difference. **DON'T FORGET YOUR MANAGERS.** They will make or break your initiative. They can be invaluable assets and can raise the level of execution exponentially if they are engaged early and in a meaningful way. Execution is all about people. Companies that know this and focus on it will be excellent at execution.

# Execute

# Checklist for Success

*Use this checklist to make sure you have done everything possible to set yourself up for success.*

- We are executing against our written project plans as planned.

- We have specific plans to engage all employees affected by our initiative.

- We have special plans to engage our middle managers.

- We have created conversation guides for department managers and supervisors to use as they help people connect their current jobs with the future.

- We have a comprehensive training plan which includes change management for all levels if necessary.

- We have utilized existing systems (such as team leaders, computer specialists, process specialists) to help move this project forward.

# Notes

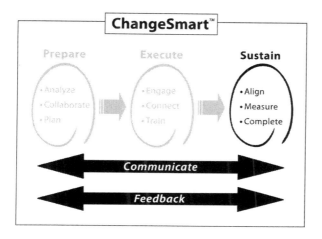

# Sustain

Sustaining a change can sometimes prove elusive in a company. Even the best laid plans can be put aside to work through a crisis or take advantage of a previously unforeseen business opportunity. It is during just those times that connecting the change you just implemented to the current crisis or business opportunity will be critical. Oftentimes, once a change is implemented the project team ceases to meet, feedback loops are no longer utilized and everyone gets back to "business as usual." "Business as usual" needs to be altered to include the new ways of operating implemented through this latest business initiative.

Sustaining a change to the business and aligning it to really come into effect is where the real ROI is achieved. Sometimes in the heat of a project the project team forgets that. In the fast paced, attention-challenged business environment of today sustaining a change can prove quite challenging. Communicating the alignment with the business and continuing to do so as the business changes isn't hard to do—it just takes someone to do it.

Often company leaders think that since the relationship is apparent and obvious to them, they don't have to verbalize it. This is a mistake. It is essential that senior management communicate even the most basic and obvious information because it may only be basic and obvious to them.

Communication is essential throughout a change initiative, but it becomes *the* vehicle during the Sustain element. As the change itself becomes "business as usual," people may forget important elements. Communication is a way of keeping those elements alive and vital.

During the Sustain element, it will be important to pay attention to:

- Alignment with the business,

- Measuring the success of the change, and

- Completing it.

# Align

No company is static, no matter what kind of business it is in. A change is implemented, but the company and the marketplace continue to evolve before, during and after the change.

It will be important for the project team, and those departments in the company who are responsible for sustaining the change, to continue showing how the change aligns with the business. One way to do this is to integrate the changes into new information that comes out. You can relate the change to updated marketing materials or show how the change continues to impact high levels of customer service. Creating those connections will help people experience the continuity so vital for a business's success.

*Case in Point:* Several months after the implementation of a new marketing strategy, a sales force was faced with unexpected bad publicity regarding one of their products. Instead of using the new strategy to plan a course of action, both marketing and the sales force abandoned all their hard work and reverted back to their old model of selling.

The steady upswing of sales they had experienced when employing the new marketing strategy disappeared and was replaced with sharply declining sales. When they realized their mistake, the sales force returned to employing the "new" marketing strategy. The sharp sales drop stopped, but no new ground was ever recovered.

If they had stayed on track with the new marketing strategy all along, would things have been different? It is impossible to know, but given the steady sales growth followed by a sharp decline, one would have to think yes.

All it would have taken was to ask one simple question—how will we handle this crisis utilizing our new marketing strategy? The answer could have guided them to take different steps.

It is precisely in times of trouble that sticking with the change you have implemented becomes essential. Aligning the unexpected market occurrence with the existing (albeit new) strategy might have saved the company from the unparalleled sales drop it experienced.

## Honor the Past to Move to the Future

There may come a time that given market forces and company responses, a business initiative that was implemented is no longer relevant. Of course, by then it is time for another change, an evolution to a more effective way of doing business. That is a natural part of doing business, and people expect it. Even then, showing how one business initiative is related to the other is an important part of the implementation strategy. The last thing people want to hear is that what they've been working so hard at up until this point has been a waste of time or, worse, has been detrimental to the business. When announcing a new business initiative or a new way of operating, avoid criticizing or discounting the previous process or insulting the previous way of doing things. People invest a lot of their time and energy into their work, and for someone to stand up and tell them it has been for naught not only creates bad feelings, it can create a morale issue that is hard to recover from.

Often in the excitement of talking about a "new" business initiative, people try to point out why it is superior to the "old" way of doing things. A better path is to show how the "old" way laid the foundation for what is about to happen. Use the opportunity to educate the employee on the evolution of the business. Show how the previous change was a necessary building block for the current direction.

People come to work every day and strive to do their best. It is always important to remember that as people search for the continuity that will lessen the negative impact of another change.

# Notes

## Measure

Although you measure how the change is impacting your business during the Sustain element, the planning for the measurements should be done during the Plan element. During the Plan element the project team should be creating measurements or metrics that answer the question: How will we know we have been successful in implementing this change? Of course, in most cases, the impact to the bottom line will be the ultimate measurement. This can be achieved through business growth or through cost savings, whatever the business initiative was meant to target.

There might also be specific metrics in regards to processes—perhaps it will take three days to get a product to market after the change compared to six days to market prior. Or perhaps after implementation, the company will only need to maintain two days of inventory to meet customer needs rather than seven.

Measurement should be one of the first things that a project team discusses. Although you may assign one person overall responsibility for measurement, it is really the task of the entire team to decide what to measure and how the team will know that success has been achieved.

We often think of metrics as a mysterious topic that only a Key Performance Indicators specialist can speak to. KPI specialists can be very helpful, and if you have the resources, by all means, engage one. However, not having the resources to hire a measurement expert shouldn't prevent you from instituting meaningful metrics.

You know what success looks like for your business. You likewise know how you'll recognize it as you look around the company. Translate that into measurements by asking the simple question: How will I know that?

The answer will tell you where your measurements will come from. For example, if success is found in an increase in sales, asking and answering the question "How will I know that sales have increased?" will give you the source of your performance.

## Baseline, Baseline, Baseline

I have talked with companies that want to cut their time to market or their inventory in half. But when asked what their current time to market is, or their current inventory, their answers are a bit vague. It is essential for a company to know where they are beginning. If you want to cut your inventory in half, that's great, but it would be better if your goal was to lower the inventory of a certain product by a certain number of days. That is cutting your inventory, but you know specifically what that means. And it can be talked about and measured easily.

Often a company will want to skip this step because the endeavor alone will take time, money and other resources. My advice is that it is money well spent. Then your success cannot be challenged. In the 80's and early 90's I saw good careers crumble because a project was done with great fanfare (and expense) but project leaders could not prove they were successful because they had no baseline numbers. Companies are a lot smarter today—they will rarely approve expenditures without knowing all the facts. But if your company hasn't learned that lesson yet, beware—and be prepared to get the facts before you begin.

# Notes

# Complete

One of the most important components in the ChangeSmart™ framework is the Complete component. Sometimes when I work with a company that has struggled through a change, the overwhelming comment is "when is this change going to be over?" It is important to keep that in mind as you carry out and try to make a change part of the standard operating procedures.

### Are We There Yet?

Another important question for the project team to answer is: "When is the project and the implementation of the change over?" There will come a time when you want the change to become part of the everyday workings of the company. Your goal in having a plan for implementing that change is to get to that day. Having a specific end date will be important. I have seen change projects fail because there was no end—the project (and the change) sadly just faded away.

This end date doesn't have to be announced, but it should be the date that the project team and eventually those who carry on the new way of doing business work towards. If you think the change will take three months to implement and then an additional three months to become part of the fabric of the company, then your end date is six months from the date implementation starts.

Your project team and your metrics will need to continue to be in place in some form until that date is passed. You may want to identify the end date based on your performance metrics—when you reach a certain level of sales or when you achieve your inventory goals and hold them for a month.

Choose criteria that are based on the reasons you decided

to make the changes to begin with. The project team should collectively decide when the end date should be. A good question to start the discussion could be "how will we know that this change has become just the way we do business?" The ensuing discussion will help you decide on your "complete" date.

*Case in Point:* Two scientifically oriented customer care departments in a company were being merged back together, after having been split apart a few years earlier. There was a project team and several integration sub-teams that were charged with making the change go as smoothly as possible. This was a very emotionally charged project. Almost everyone who was about to be merged together had also been through the split. They were upset when the split occurred and were now even more upset when the merger was announced.

The project team was well aware of these issues when they met for the first time and considered the context into which this change was being put into action. Throughout the merger the teams met consistently to plan and change course if necessary. The consistency of team membership and regular meetings kept everyone energized and focused on the goals.

Even though the merger was fraught with emotion, the teams did a good job of handling what came up effectively. Senior management and team leaders took complete control of communicating everything to the employees. The team worked out any issues before they were brought to the general employee population. This helped all employees understand the thought process of the team and senior management.

The team had set a date of six months from the date activities started to the date the project would end. Team members kept the end date in mind as they planned activities and thought about timing. The date wasn't set arbitrarily. The team had talked long and hard about what was realistic before anything was even announced. Six months seemed long enough to complete the work without dragging the project on.

The goal of a complete merger within 6 months was met, and it positioned the new department well for additional changes that happened afterwards. (They were merged several months later with another customer care group within their family of companies.)

The consistency of team membership during the entire project really helped this initiative succeed as did focusing on the project end date. Without that end date critical activities could have been put off as the departments struggled to continue "business as usual" for their customers while doing the additional merger work. It is a good example of what can be achieved when an end date is identified and a project team isn't a revolving door. Having an end date helped that as well—people knew the project was finite and wouldn't "linger," so they could sign up to be a part of it for the entire time.

As you think about putting together project teams, keep in mind that the longer the team can remain intact, the better your results will be. Changes should be expected on longer term projects—but planning for them and managing them will be critical.

The monetary value of having the same people that made the decisions implement them may be hard to measure, but we all know results are better when that happens.

If you do have to make a change, make sure the new person or persons understand the history of decisions and the reasoning behind them so they can start working productively as soon as possible. It will be natural for new folks to question what they weren't present for, but it needs to be managed so the project doesn't get off track. The end date is one of those decisions that should be understood by new project team members. The end date is always chosen for a reason and needs to be fully documented and explained.

## A Tool You Can Use: Lessons Learned

Full implementation of a new business initiative is a cause for celebration and reflection. Conducting a Lessons Learned session and combining that with a team celebration is a great way to end a change initiative.

A typical Lessons Learned session will give people a chance to comment on what went well and what they would do differently next time. This can be done in a variety of ways, but however you choose to do it, give people a chance to voice their thoughts anonymously. It will be important to invite all members of the project team to the meeting. Don't leave anyone out just because you might not like what that person has to say. It may also be beneficial to include additional business partners.

A typical Lessons Learned session can go like this:

1. Set ground rules about confidentiality and fairness.

2. Using Flipcharts and post-it notes (for anonymity), start the conversation at the general level: what went well, what you'd do over if you had the chance.

   - You may want to categorize the project by stages or topics and then give people a chance to answer those basic questions under those categories.

3. Once general comments have been gathered, assign team members to different flipcharts and ask them to create additional questions to be answered or topics to be discussed.

4. Keeping the information intact on the original flipcharts, create new flipcharts and repeat the process if desired. If not, go to the next step.

5. Engage the group in a discussion on the one or two areas that may need additional clarification. If the group is large, you may want to break down into smaller groups. Make sure there is a note taker throughout all discussions.

The information gathered during a Lessons Learned helps the team learn for the future and also becomes the basis for organizational learning. Using the Lessons Learned from previous projects can help new project teams jump start their way to success.

Store your Lessons Learned in a central place—electronically or otherwise. Make your triumphs and insights available for others to learn from in the months and years to come. Don't gloss over the struggles, otherwise others won't be able to learn from them.

# Sustain

# Checklist for Success

*Use this checklist to make sure you have done everything possible to set yourself up for success.*

- We continue to show how our business initiative aligns to the business through verbal and written communication.

- We have discussed and set up specific measurements to track our progress toward our goals.

- We know when we want to close down the project and have set a project end date.

- We are honoring our past as we continue to focus on our future.

- We have conducted a lessons learned meeting and have shared the results.

# Notes

# Resistance

No book on change management would be complete without a discussion on resistance. It is missing on the preceding pages because I know from experience that the better a change is managed, the less resistance you will have. But all change causes some level of resistance in people, and it is always better to be prepared.

Resistance is a word fraught with emotions. You probably never think of it as good. That is until now.

Resistance you know about is actually a gift. People are willingly sharing their discomfort about a planned change and therefore are giving you a chance to relieve it. That is truly a gift!

As you have probably seen from your own experience, not all resistance is the same. Some is intense and without reason; some is cold and calculated filled with facts and figures. Different types of resistance require different responses. Once you know how to identify and respond to different types of resistance, it will be easier for you to treat it like the gift it is.

Resistance tells you that there is a problem of some kind with your proposed business change and you are being given the opportunity to partner with the resisting group or individual to solve the problem. The alternative is that the resistor(s) will go "underground"—still resisting, just not telling you. This can undermine your efforts every step of the way. And resistance unresolved is resistance that grows. If you announce a new business strategy and there is no resistance, be concerned. Be very concerned.

Smart leaders seek out resistance. They know that there are many smart people in their organizations and all of them couldn't be in the room when the decision was made. By seeking out those people who have a critical view of the business, a leader can refine and improve their business strategy. At the very least, smart business leaders listen to the voices of resistance and try to really understand what is being said.

*"Resistance you know about is a gift."*

**Three Types of Resistance**

Resistance can be the most challenging part of a change effort. In order to approach resistance and resistors productively, it is helpful to understand that all resistance is ***not*** the same. Our first instinct may be to try to force resisters into going along with our plans. Or we try to discourage resistance by cutting off all voices of concern. Neither of these tactics will ultimately be successful.

Since all resistance is not the same, different approaches are needed depending on the type of resistance encountered. When encountering someone you consider "resistant," probe first to make sure the individual is, in fact, resisting. S/He may just be voicing concerns, which when answered could alleviate their "resistance." Resistance can occur in both a positive and a negative change and will completely depend on the individual's view.

In the late 90's I heard Columbia Professor and change expert W. Warner Burke speak about three categories of change at a conference: Blind, Ideological and Political Resistance. Finally someone put into words what I had been feeling all along! Over the years I have found these categories quite useful in understanding that all change is not the same and should be treated accordingly. My definitions and experiences within these groupings may depart from Burke's but the spirit remains the same. [1]

**Blind Resistance**

The first type of resistance is typically very hard for manager's to handle. Blind resistance is resisting with little reasoning or logic behind it. A person might say "I think this is the wrong way to go," and when asked why, may not have a very good answer, or any answer at all. Blind resistance is sometimes seen as a result of nonstop, significant change. Individuals have a limit to how much change they can absorb successfully. Blind resistance is a way of saying "ENOUGH"!

The best way to approach an individual who is exhibiting Blind Resistance is to back off initially and wait a bit. It is not uncommon to see managers faced with blind resistance pull rank and tell the individual to just accept the changes and move on. Oftentimes these individuals are branded "resistant" and treated accordingly. That will not do the company and certainly not the individual any good. By backing off initially and waiting a bit, you are giving the individual a chance to get over his or her initial feelings and begin to see things differently. Come back to the resistant party and initiate a dialogue with them about the proposed changes. Ask them to tell you, from their perspective, what the worst thing that could happen to the company would be if the changes went ahead as planned. Ask them what the worst thing that could happen to them would be. Then ask them what they would do.

By allowing the persons exhibiting Blind Resistance to verbalize their 'worst case scenario' you are encouraging them to share their thought process with you. That helps them because a 'worst case scenario' rarely happens, but if it does, they've already started thinking about their 'plan b.' It helps you to see how they interpreted what they heard about the change, and since they probably aren't the only individuals who heard it that way, it will help you refine your future communications on this topic.

**Ideological Resistance**

Ideological Resistance is when people don't agree with the proposed change and have logical and cogent arguments to support their position. Their resistance usually sounds reasonable and well thought out. It would not be out of the ordinary to hear Ideological Resistance among your 'best and brightest.' After all, you hired them for their business abilities, and it would be natural for them to look at the information available to them and have a different opinion.

When you are approaching a party showing Ideological Resistance, make sure you understand their arguments. That means that if they quote a source or two, look into it. Initiate a conversation with them solely for the purpose of understanding their point of view. Don't just take down the points of their argument so you can refute them later. That will defeat the purpose of the conversation.

Once you understand their argument, acknowledge their point of view. If they have taken the time to have a well thought out and organized opinion, acknowledging their view will go a long way in mitigating their resistance. Be honest with yourself and them. There are usually many different options when making a business decision. The one you choose is the best one for the current circumstances but isn't usually the only option out there. They may think their idea is best because they don't look at the organization and the business from the same vantage point you do.

The last step in moving this category of resistor over to your 'side' is to help them understand your decision from your vantage point. Lay out your argument logically and convincingly. Sometimes that is all that is needed to help an Ideological Resistor move on.

## Political Resistance

The last of the three categories of resistance is one often called "Political." It could also be called 'Loss Resistance' because it is found when there is a perceived or real loss of something important or significant to that individual. The way Political Resistance shows itself is in the language people use as they talk about it. It may sound like this: "Oh well, I can kiss my promotion goodbye now." "Dr. Jones is going to be so mad. I'm the fourth sales rep he's had this year." "I can't believe I won't be doing that part of my job anymore; I really liked doing that."

A perceived loss will obviously need to be handled differently than a real loss. And loss of a job is a whole other category.

A perceived loss can be shown to be otherwise by allowing the individuals to talk about what that loss is. Once you know what they think they are losing, it will be easier to help them see that that is not so. Or it will be easier to give them ideas on how to minimize that perceived loss.

A real loss such as losing a manager or a chance to work on a specific project can cause persons to resist the change indefinitely. It is best to help them see how even though they may be losing something tangible in the short-term, that there are many more opportunities in the long-term.

Losing a manager is usually a real loss that brings about a perceived loss—loss of a chance for promotion, loss of a chance to work on a special project. You can't make the real loss go away, but you can help resistant party gain some perspective. Dialogue with them about what they are not losing or what is not changing for them. Ask them what they are losing or giving up that they are happy about (it could happen). Help them focus on what they can control and can't control as a way of giving the change some context. All of these questions and the dialogue that ensues will help this person move past their Political Resistance much quicker.

Buying into the myth that resistance is bad will not help your business strategy succeed. Seeing resistance as a gift and understanding the different types of resistance will give you a chance to use all the information available. As you use that information, you will be creating a foundation of success for this change, and for all future changes you will make.

# Conclusion

You are at the end already! As you read through the different elements of the ChangeSmart™ framework, I hope you discovered that you already do some of what is in this book. I also hope you realized that with just a little effort you can implement much of what was talked about.

A company's ability to make effective changes will be the difference between success and failure in the 21$^{st}$ century. Change management, helping organizations reach their desired state through people, will continue to be an essential component of this. There doesn't have to be anything magic about implementing change as long as you keep a few simple things in mind:

- Plan for it

- Execute it as planned

- Sustain it

- Communicate

- Gather feedback along the way

Simple, yes, but each requires attention and effort. Just as with anything else in a business, wishing will not make your initiative successful. Miracles don't happen as much as we want them to.

Using the ChangeSmart™ framework will make the attention and effort you put into making your business initiative successful infinitely easier and definitely more fruitful.

Good luck!

# Endnotes

[1] For those interested, W. Warner Burke subsequently published a textbook on change in 2002 called Organization Change: Theory and Practice.

# Index

ChangeSmart™: Implementing Change Without Lowering Your Bottom Line

Align 47
Analyze 5, 6
Barriers 12, 13, 14
Blind Resistance 63, 64
Collaborate 16
Complete 54
Connect 33
Conversation Guide 34, 42
Enablers 12, 13, 14
Engage 29
Execute 27, 67
Feedback Loop 16, 17, 18, 26
Ideological Resistance 64
Lessons Learned 57, 58, 59
Loss 66
Middle Management Alert 9, 11, 17, 20, 35, 40
Measurement 52
Organizational Attention Span 28
Political Resistance 65
Resigning in Place 35
Resistance 61, 62, 66
ROI xii, 45
Sustain 45, 46, 59, 67
Train 36, 39
Work Identity 34

Made in the USA
Lexington, KY
02 September 2011